OUR FAMILY

— ◆ ❖ ◆ —

A FILL-IN BOOK OF TRADITIONS,
MEMORIES, AND STORIES

THIS BOOK BELONGS TO:

_____

"I do think that families are the most beautiful things in all the world!"

LOUISA MAY ALCOTT, *LITTLE WOMEN*

MAKE THIS BOOK YOURS

START WITH YOUR IMMEDIATE FAMILY.

Record details and memories about the people you share your day-to-day life with. There is space to paste in a few favorite snapshots, write about your favorite household traditions, and more.

CREATE A TIME CAPSULE WITH THE REPEATING QUESTIONNAIRES.

Capture fun facts, favorite stories, and memories from individual family members by passing around this book at big celebrations, like a family reunion or another large gathering of your extended family. You can also use the questionnaires with just your immediate family, returning to the book regularly at birthdays or holidays as a fun way to chart how everyone has grown and changed as time has passed.

GET TOGETHER WITH A GAME.

Invite the whole family to participate as a group with some fun games and activities that tease out interesting facts and stories about everyone in the room. Some are meant to be read aloud, and other activities work best if the book is passed around among family members.

NO MATTER HOW YOU USE THIS BOOK, YOU'LL HAVE A BEAUTIFUL COLLECTION OF FAMILY MEMORIES TO TREASURE FOR YEARS TO COME.

· 1 ·

OUR IMMEDIATE FAMILY

▸▸ ◆ ◂◂

This first chapter is devoted to those closest to you:
the members of your immediate family. The activities
that follow capture the essence of this core group of
people and celebrate the unique memories, traditions,
and qualities that define your household.

WHO WE ARE

LIST YOUR FAMILY MEMBERS' NAMES AND AGES BELOW.

PARENT(S)

_____

_____

_____

CHILDREN

_____

_____

_____

DOES ANYONE ELSE LIVE WITH YOU? MAYBE A GRANDPARENT
OR ANOTHER RELATIVE? PUT THEIR NAMES HERE.

_____

_____

_____

ANY ANIMAL FRIENDS SHARING YOUR HOME? LIST YOUR PETS HERE!

_____

_____

_____

DESCRIBE YOUR HOME. WHAT KIND OF PLACE DO YOU LIVE IN?
HOW LONG HAVE YOU BEEN THERE? IS THERE ANYTHING ABOUT
YOUR HOME THAT MAKES IT SPECIAL TO YOUR FAMILY?

_____

_____

_____

_____

_____

_____

_____

_____

WHAT ABOUT THE NEIGHBORHOOD? WHAT ARE THE THINGS
ABOUT YOUR HOMETOWN YOUR FAMILY ENJOYS THE MOST?

_____

_____

_____

_____

_____

_____

_____

_____

_____

FAMILY PORTRAIT

◆ ◦⬩◦ ◆

Your family is unlike any other. It's made up of unique individuals
who all come together to form an extraordinary whole.

PASTE YOUR FAVORITE FAMILY PHOTO IN THE SPACE BELOW. WHERE WAS IT TAKEN? WHAT MAKES IT YOUR FAVORITE? WRITE A SHORT CAPTION TO SET THE SCENE.

_____

_____

_____

_____

_____

_____

PHOTO GALLERY

◆ ◆ ◆

A picture is worth a thousand words, and photos can capture
special moments and memories in ways words never will.

PASTE SOME OF YOUR FAVORITE FAMILY SNAPSHOTS HERE.

FAMILY TREE

———————————— ◆ ————————————

Families come in all shapes and sizes. Whether your family
has many branches, or just a few, each one is special.

USE THE SPACE BELOW TO DRAW A FAMILY TREE. START WITH YOUR IMMEDIATE FAMILY AND ADD BRANCHES FOR AS MANY GENERATIONS AS YOU WANT TO INCLUDE.

OUR ANCESTRY

What do you know about your family's background? Where do you come from? How did everyone end up where they are today?

WRITE DOWN WHAT YOU KNOW HERE.

_____

_____

_____

_____

_____

_____

_____

_____

_____

_____

_____

_____

_____

_____

_____

FAMILY LORE

Does your family have any stories that have been passed down?
Any notable ancestors, family legends, or superstitions that everyone gets told?

WRITE YOUR STORIES HERE.

COAT OF ARMS

◆

In medieval times, noble families identified themselves
to the world with a coat of arms, an emblem used to express
their family's particular characteristics and achievements.
What aspects of your family set it apart from others?

DESIGN A COAT OF ARMS THAT REPRESENTS YOUR FAMILY
AND COME UP WITH A MOTTO TO PUT IN THE BANNER BELOW.

IDEAS: TRY DIVIDING THE SHIELD INTO QUARTERS AND DECORATING EACH PIECE WITH A SYMBOL THAT
REPRESENTS YOUR FAMILY'S FAVORITE ACTIVITIES (LIKE A BOOK FOR READING OR A CAMPFIRE FOR CAMPING)
OR CREATE A STRIPE FOR EACH FAMILY MEMBER AND COLOR IT IN WITH THEIR FAVORITE COLOR.

HOLIDAY TRADITIONS

How does your family celebrate the holidays? What do you look forward to the most? Are there any rituals you've been practicing for years?

WRITE DOWN YOUR FAMILY'S FAVORITE HOLIDAY TRADITIONS.

QUESTIONNAIRES

▸◆◂

In this chapter, each family member has the opportunity to record fun facts about themselves and share their favorite stories and personal memories by filling out a questionnaire. If you're having a reunion or another large gathering of your extended family, you can pass the book around so each person can fill in a questionnaire and create a record of who they are and what their thoughts are on that particular day. Alternatively, you can use this section with just your immediate family and return to the book annually at birthdays or holidays, using the questionnaires as a fun way to record how everyone has changed over time.

NAME

NICKNAME

DATE

AGE

OCCASION

I WOULD DESCRIBE MYSELF AS . . .

MY FAMILY WOULD DESCRIBE ME AS . . .

WHAT I ATE FOR BREAKFAST THIS MORNING:

WHAT I'M WEARING TODAY:

WHAT I'M CURRENTLY WATCHING:

WHAT I'M CURRENTLY LISTENING TO:

WHAT I'M CURRENTLY READING:

THE LAST PERSON I TALKED TO:

_____

THE LAST PERSON I TEXTED:

_____

IF I COULD BE INTRODUCED TO ANYONE, I'D WANT TO MEET . . .

_____

IF I COULD GO ANYWHERE TOMORROW, I'D VISIT . . .

_____

SOMEDAY, I WANT TO . . .

_____

I'M MOST GRATEFUL FOR . . .

_____

MY FAVORITE FAMILY STORY:

_____

_____

_____

SOMETHING ABOUT THIS DAY I'LL ALWAYS REMEMBER:

_____

_____

_____

NAME

NICKNAME

DATE

AGE

OCCASION

I WOULD DESCRIBE MYSELF AS . . .

MY FAMILY WOULD DESCRIBE ME AS . . .

WHAT I ATE FOR BREAKFAST THIS MORNING:

WHAT I'M WEARING TODAY:

WHAT I'M CURRENTLY WATCHING:

WHAT I'M CURRENTLY LISTENING TO:

WHAT I'M CURRENTLY READING:

THE LAST PERSON I TALKED TO:

_____

THE LAST PERSON I TEXTED:

_____

IF I COULD BE INTRODUCED TO ANYONE, I'D WANT TO MEET . . .

_____

IF I COULD GO ANYWHERE TOMORROW, I'D VISIT . . .

_____

SOMEDAY, I WANT TO . . .

_____

I'M MOST GRATEFUL FOR . . .

_____

MY FAVORITE FAMILY STORY:

_____

_____

_____

SOMETHING ABOUT THIS DAY I'LL ALWAYS REMEMBER:

_____

_____

_____

NAME

NICKNAME

DATE

AGE

OCCASION

I WOULD DESCRIBE MYSELF AS . . .

MY FAMILY WOULD DESCRIBE ME AS . . .

WHAT I ATE FOR BREAKFAST THIS MORNING:

WHAT I'M WEARING TODAY:

WHAT I'M CURRENTLY WATCHING:

WHAT I'M CURRENTLY LISTENING TO:

WHAT I'M CURRENTLY READING:

THE LAST PERSON I TALKED TO:

_____

THE LAST PERSON I TEXTED:

_____

IF I COULD BE INTRODUCED TO ANYONE, I'D WANT TO MEET . . .

_____

IF I COULD GO ANYWHERE TOMORROW, I'D VISIT . . .

_____

SOMEDAY, I WANT TO . . .

_____

I'M MOST GRATEFUL FOR . . .

_____

MY FAVORITE FAMILY STORY:

_____

_____

_____

SOMETHING ABOUT THIS DAY I'LL ALWAYS REMEMBER:

_____

_____

_____

NAME

NICKNAME

DATE

AGE

OCCASION

I WOULD DESCRIBE MYSELF AS . . .

_____

MY FAMILY WOULD DESCRIBE ME AS . . .

_____

WHAT I ATE FOR BREAKFAST THIS MORNING:

_____

WHAT I'M WEARING TODAY:

_____

WHAT I'M CURRENTLY WATCHING:

_____

WHAT I'M CURRENTLY LISTENING TO:

_____

WHAT I'M CURRENTLY READING:

_____

THE LAST PERSON I TALKED TO:

_____

THE LAST PERSON I TEXTED:

_____

IF I COULD BE INTRODUCED TO ANYONE, I'D WANT TO MEET . . .

_____

IF I COULD GO ANYWHERE TOMORROW, I'D VISIT . . .

_____

SOMEDAY, I WANT TO . . .

_____

I'M MOST GRATEFUL FOR . . .

_____

MY FAVORITE FAMILY STORY:

_____

_____

_____

SOMETHING ABOUT THIS DAY I'LL ALWAYS REMEMBER:

_____

_____

_____

Clan ('klan), *n.*

From Gaelic *clann* offspring, descendants;
akin to Irish *clann*, *cland*, offspring, tribe, family;

1.

A tribe or collection of families, united under a chieftain, regarded as having the same common ancestor, and bearing the same surname; as, the *clan* of Macdonald.

2.

A clique; a sect, society, or body of persons; esp., a body of persons united by some common interest or pursuit.

NAME

NICKNAME

DATE

AGE

OCCASION

I WOULD DESCRIBE MYSELF AS . . .

MY FAMILY WOULD DESCRIBE ME AS . . .

WHAT I ATE FOR BREAKFAST THIS MORNING:

WHAT I'M WEARING TODAY:

WHAT I'M CURRENTLY WATCHING:

WHAT I'M CURRENTLY LISTENING TO:

WHAT I'M CURRENTLY READING:

THE LAST PERSON I TALKED TO:

_____

THE LAST PERSON I TEXTED:

_____

IF I COULD BE INTRODUCED TO ANYONE, I'D WANT TO MEET . . .

_____

IF I COULD GO ANYWHERE TOMORROW, I'D VISIT . . .

_____

SOMEDAY, I WANT TO . . .

_____

I'M MOST GRATEFUL FOR . . .

_____

MY FAVORITE FAMILY STORY:

_____

_____

_____

SOMETHING ABOUT THIS DAY I'LL ALWAYS REMEMBER:

_____

_____

_____

NAME

NICKNAME

DATE

AGE

OCCASION

I WOULD DESCRIBE MYSELF AS . . .

_____

MY FAMILY WOULD DESCRIBE ME AS . . .

_____

WHAT I ATE FOR BREAKFAST THIS MORNING:

_____

WHAT I'M WEARING TODAY:

_____

WHAT I'M CURRENTLY WATCHING:

_____

WHAT I'M CURRENTLY LISTENING TO:

_____

WHAT I'M CURRENTLY READING:

_____

THE LAST PERSON I TALKED TO:

_____

THE LAST PERSON I TEXTED:

_____

IF I COULD BE INTRODUCED TO ANYONE, I'D WANT TO MEET . . .

_____

IF I COULD GO ANYWHERE TOMORROW, I'D VISIT . . .

_____

SOMEDAY, I WANT TO . . .

_____

I'M MOST GRATEFUL FOR . . .

_____

MY FAVORITE FAMILY STORY:

_____

_____

_____

SOMETHING ABOUT THIS DAY I'LL ALWAYS REMEMBER:

_____

_____

_____

NAME

NICKNAME

DATE

AGE

OCCASION

I WOULD DESCRIBE MYSELF AS . . .

MY FAMILY WOULD DESCRIBE ME AS . . .

WHAT I ATE FOR BREAKFAST THIS MORNING:

WHAT I'M WEARING TODAY:

WHAT I'M CURRENTLY WATCHING:

WHAT I'M CURRENTLY LISTENING TO:

WHAT I'M CURRENTLY READING:

THE LAST PERSON I TALKED TO:

_____

THE LAST PERSON I TEXTED:

_____

IF I COULD BE INTRODUCED TO ANYONE, I'D WANT TO MEET . . .

_____

IF I COULD GO ANYWHERE TOMORROW, I'D VISIT . . .

_____

SOMEDAY, I WANT TO . . .

_____

I'M MOST GRATEFUL FOR . . .

_____

MY FAVORITE FAMILY STORY:

_____

_____

_____

SOMETHING ABOUT THIS DAY I'LL ALWAYS REMEMBER:

_____

_____

_____

NAME

NICKNAME

DATE

AGE

OCCASION

I WOULD DESCRIBE MYSELF AS . . .

_____

MY FAMILY WOULD DESCRIBE ME AS . . .

_____

WHAT I ATE FOR BREAKFAST THIS MORNING:

_____

WHAT I'M WEARING TODAY:

_____

WHAT I'M CURRENTLY WATCHING:

_____

WHAT I'M CURRENTLY LISTENING TO:

_____

WHAT I'M CURRENTLY READING:

_____

THE LAST PERSON I TALKED TO:

_____

THE LAST PERSON I TEXTED:

_____

IF I COULD BE INTRODUCED TO ANYONE, I'D WANT TO MEET . . .

_____

IF I COULD GO ANYWHERE TOMORROW, I'D VISIT . . .

_____

SOMEDAY, I WANT TO . . .

_____

I'M MOST GRATEFUL FOR . . .

_____

MY FAVORITE FAMILY STORY:

_____

_____

_____

SOMETHING ABOUT THIS DAY I'LL ALWAYS REMEMBER:

_____

_____

_____

NAME

NICKNAME

DATE

AGE

OCCASION

I WOULD DESCRIBE MYSELF AS . . .

MY FAMILY WOULD DESCRIBE ME AS . . .

WHAT I ATE FOR BREAKFAST THIS MORNING:

WHAT I'M WEARING TODAY:

WHAT I'M CURRENTLY WATCHING:

WHAT I'M CURRENTLY LISTENING TO:

WHAT I'M CURRENTLY READING:

THE LAST PERSON I TALKED TO:

_____

THE LAST PERSON I TEXTED:

_____

IF I COULD BE INTRODUCED TO ANYONE, I'D WANT TO MEET . . .

_____

IF I COULD GO ANYWHERE TOMORROW, I'D VISIT . . .

_____

SOMEDAY, I WANT TO . . .

_____

I'M MOST GRATEFUL FOR . . .

_____

MY FAVORITE FAMILY STORY:

_____

_____

_____

SOMETHING ABOUT THIS DAY I'LL ALWAYS REMEMBER:

_____

_____

_____

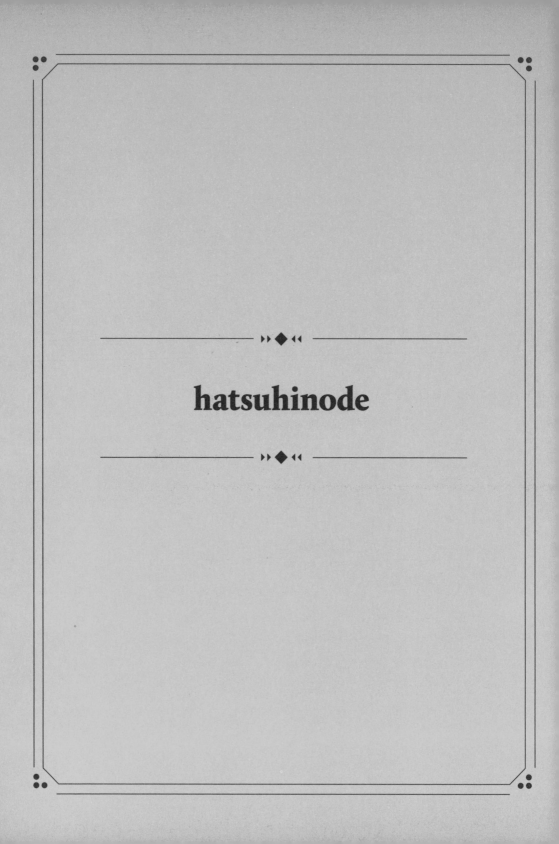

hatsuhinode

In Japan, the first sunrise of the year, or *hatsuhinode*, carries special significance and is thought to bring luck to whoever views it. Early on New Year's Day, families gather to greet the sun and celebrate the start of another year together.

NAME

NICKNAME

DATE

AGE

OCCASION

I WOULD DESCRIBE MYSELF AS . . .

_____

MY FAMILY WOULD DESCRIBE ME AS . . .

_____

WHAT I ATE FOR BREAKFAST THIS MORNING:

_____

WHAT I'M WEARING TODAY:

_____

WHAT I'M CURRENTLY WATCHING:

_____

WHAT I'M CURRENTLY LISTENING TO:

_____

WHAT I'M CURRENTLY READING:

_____

THE LAST PERSON I TALKED TO:

_____

THE LAST PERSON I TEXTED:

_____

IF I COULD BE INTRODUCED TO ANYONE, I'D WANT TO MEET . . .

_____

IF I COULD GO ANYWHERE TOMORROW, I'D VISIT . . .

_____

SOMEDAY, I WANT TO . . .

_____

I'M MOST GRATEFUL FOR . . .

_____

MY FAVORITE FAMILY STORY:

_____

_____

_____

SOMETHING ABOUT THIS DAY I'LL ALWAYS REMEMBER:

_____

_____

_____

NAME

NICKNAME

DATE

AGE

OCCASION

I WOULD DESCRIBE MYSELF AS . . .

_____

MY FAMILY WOULD DESCRIBE ME AS . . .

_____

WHAT I ATE FOR BREAKFAST THIS MORNING:

_____

WHAT I'M WEARING TODAY:

_____

WHAT I'M CURRENTLY WATCHING:

_____

WHAT I'M CURRENTLY LISTENING TO:

_____

WHAT I'M CURRENTLY READING:

_____

THE LAST PERSON I TALKED TO:

_____

THE LAST PERSON I TEXTED:

_____

IF I COULD BE INTRODUCED TO ANYONE, I'D WANT TO MEET . . .

_____

IF I COULD GO ANYWHERE TOMORROW, I'D VISIT . . .

_____

SOMEDAY, I WANT TO . . .

_____

I'M MOST GRATEFUL FOR . . .

_____

MY FAVORITE FAMILY STORY:

_____

_____

_____

SOMETHING ABOUT THIS DAY I'LL ALWAYS REMEMBER:

_____

_____

_____

NAME

NICKNAME

DATE

AGE

OCCASION

I WOULD DESCRIBE MYSELF AS . . .

_____

MY FAMILY WOULD DESCRIBE ME AS . . .

_____

WHAT I ATE FOR BREAKFAST THIS MORNING:

_____

WHAT I'M WEARING TODAY:

_____

WHAT I'M CURRENTLY WATCHING:

_____

WHAT I'M CURRENTLY LISTENING TO:

_____

WHAT I'M CURRENTLY READING:

_____

THE LAST PERSON I TALKED TO:

_____

THE LAST PERSON I TEXTED:

_____

IF I COULD BE INTRODUCED TO ANYONE, I'D WANT TO MEET . . .

_____

IF I COULD GO ANYWHERE TOMORROW, I'D VISIT . . .

_____

SOMEDAY, I WANT TO . . .

_____

I'M MOST GRATEFUL FOR . . .

_____

MY FAVORITE FAMILY STORY:

_____

_____

_____

SOMETHING ABOUT THIS DAY I'LL ALWAYS REMEMBER:

_____

_____

_____

NAME

NICKNAME

DATE

AGE

OCCASION

I WOULD DESCRIBE MYSELF AS . . .

MY FAMILY WOULD DESCRIBE ME AS . . .

WHAT I ATE FOR BREAKFAST THIS MORNING:

WHAT I'M WEARING TODAY:

WHAT I'M CURRENTLY WATCHING:

WHAT I'M CURRENTLY LISTENING TO:

WHAT I'M CURRENTLY READING:

THE LAST PERSON I TALKED TO:

_____

THE LAST PERSON I TEXTED:

_____

IF I COULD BE INTRODUCED TO ANYONE, I'D WANT TO MEET . . .

_____

IF I COULD GO ANYWHERE TOMORROW, I'D VISIT . . .

_____

SOMEDAY, I WANT TO . . .

_____

I'M MOST GRATEFUL FOR . . .

_____

MY FAVORITE FAMILY STORY:

_____

_____

_____

SOMETHING ABOUT THIS DAY I'LL ALWAYS REMEMBER:

_____

_____

_____

NAME

NICKNAME

DATE

AGE

OCCASION

I WOULD DESCRIBE MYSELF AS . . .

MY FAMILY WOULD DESCRIBE ME AS . . .

WHAT I ATE FOR BREAKFAST THIS MORNING:

WHAT I'M WEARING TODAY:

WHAT I'M CURRENTLY WATCHING:

WHAT I'M CURRENTLY LISTENING TO:

WHAT I'M CURRENTLY READING:

THE LAST PERSON I TALKED TO:

_____

THE LAST PERSON I TEXTED:

_____

IF I COULD BE INTRODUCED TO ANYONE, I'D WANT TO MEET . . .

_____

IF I COULD GO ANYWHERE TOMORROW, I'D VISIT . . .

_____

SOMEDAY, I WANT TO . . .

_____

I'M MOST GRATEFUL FOR . . .

_____

MY FAVORITE FAMILY STORY:

_____

_____

_____

SOMETHING ABOUT THIS DAY I'LL ALWAYS REMEMBER:

_____

_____

_____

schultüte

This German tradition celebrates a child's first day of school. Every autumn, children receive a decorated paper cone, or *schultüte*, filled with school supplies, candy, and other small gifts meant to get them excited for the start of the school year.

NAME

NICKNAME

DATE

AGE

OCCASION

I WOULD DESCRIBE MYSELF AS . . .

MY FAMILY WOULD DESCRIBE ME AS . . .

WHAT I ATE FOR BREAKFAST THIS MORNING:

WHAT I'M WEARING TODAY:

WHAT I'M CURRENTLY WATCHING:

WHAT I'M CURRENTLY LISTENING TO:

WHAT I'M CURRENTLY READING:

THE LAST PERSON I TALKED TO:

_____

THE LAST PERSON I TEXTED:

_____

IF I COULD BE INTRODUCED TO ANYONE, I'D WANT TO MEET . . .

_____

IF I COULD GO ANYWHERE TOMORROW, I'D VISIT . . .

_____

SOMEDAY, I WANT TO . . .

_____

I'M MOST GRATEFUL FOR . . .

_____

MY FAVORITE FAMILY STORY:

_____

_____

_____

SOMETHING ABOUT THIS DAY I'LL ALWAYS REMEMBER:

_____

_____

_____

NAME

NICKNAME

DATE

AGE

OCCASION

I WOULD DESCRIBE MYSELF AS . . .

_____

MY FAMILY WOULD DESCRIBE ME AS . . .

_____

WHAT I ATE FOR BREAKFAST THIS MORNING:

_____

WHAT I'M WEARING TODAY:

_____

WHAT I'M CURRENTLY WATCHING:

_____

WHAT I'M CURRENTLY LISTENING TO:

_____

WHAT I'M CURRENTLY READING:

_____

THE LAST PERSON I TALKED TO:

_____

THE LAST PERSON I TEXTED:

_____

IF I COULD BE INTRODUCED TO ANYONE, I'D WANT TO MEET . . .

_____

IF I COULD GO ANYWHERE TOMORROW, I'D VISIT . . .

_____

SOMEDAY, I WANT TO . . .

_____

I'M MOST GRATEFUL FOR . . .

_____

MY FAVORITE FAMILY STORY:

_____

_____

_____

SOMETHING ABOUT THIS DAY I'LL ALWAYS REMEMBER:

_____

_____

_____

NAME

NICKNAME

DATE

AGE

OCCASION

I WOULD DESCRIBE MYSELF AS . . .

_____

MY FAMILY WOULD DESCRIBE ME AS . . .

_____

WHAT I ATE FOR BREAKFAST THIS MORNING:

_____

WHAT I'M WEARING TODAY:

_____

WHAT I'M CURRENTLY WATCHING:

_____

WHAT I'M CURRENTLY LISTENING TO:

_____

WHAT I'M CURRENTLY READING:

_____

THE LAST PERSON I TALKED TO:

_____

THE LAST PERSON I TEXTED:

_____

IF I COULD BE INTRODUCED TO ANYONE, I'D WANT TO MEET . . .

_____

IF I COULD GO ANYWHERE TOMORROW, I'D VISIT . . .

_____

SOMEDAY, I WANT TO . . .

_____

I'M MOST GRATEFUL FOR . . .

_____

MY FAVORITE FAMILY STORY:

_____

_____

_____

SOMETHING ABOUT THIS DAY I'LL ALWAYS REMEMBER:

_____

_____

_____

NAME

NICKNAME

DATE

AGE

OCCASION

I WOULD DESCRIBE MYSELF AS . . .

_____

MY FAMILY WOULD DESCRIBE ME AS . . .

_____

WHAT I ATE FOR BREAKFAST THIS MORNING:

_____

WHAT I'M WEARING TODAY:

_____

WHAT I'M CURRENTLY WATCHING:

_____

WHAT I'M CURRENTLY LISTENING TO:

_____

WHAT I'M CURRENTLY READING:

_____

THE LAST PERSON I TALKED TO:

_____

THE LAST PERSON I TEXTED:

_____

IF I COULD BE INTRODUCED TO ANYONE, I'D WANT TO MEET . . .

_____

IF I COULD GO ANYWHERE TOMORROW, I'D VISIT . . .

_____

SOMEDAY, I WANT TO . . .

_____

I'M MOST GRATEFUL FOR . . .

_____

MY FAVORITE FAMILY STORY:

_____

_____

_____

SOMETHING ABOUT THIS DAY I'LL ALWAYS REMEMBER:

_____

_____

_____

NAME

NICKNAME

DATE

AGE

OCCASION

I WOULD DESCRIBE MYSELF AS . . .

MY FAMILY WOULD DESCRIBE ME AS . . .

WHAT I ATE FOR BREAKFAST THIS MORNING:

WHAT I'M WEARING TODAY:

WHAT I'M CURRENTLY WATCHING:

WHAT I'M CURRENTLY LISTENING TO:

WHAT I'M CURRENTLY READING:

THE LAST PERSON I TALKED TO:

_____

THE LAST PERSON I TEXTED:

_____

IF I COULD BE INTRODUCED TO ANYONE, I'D WANT TO MEET . . .

_____

IF I COULD GO ANYWHERE TOMORROW, I'D VISIT . . .

_____

SOMEDAY, I WANT TO . . .

_____

I'M MOST GRATEFUL FOR . . .

_____

MY FAVORITE FAMILY STORY:

_____

_____

_____

SOMETHING ABOUT THIS DAY I'LL ALWAYS REMEMBER:

_____

_____

_____

Kin ('kin) *n.*

From Old English *kin*, *cun*, *cynn* kin, kind,
race, people; akin to *cennan* to beget;

I.

Relationship, consanguinity, or affinity;
connection by birth or marriage; kindred;
near connection or alliance, as of those
having common descent.

2.

Relatives; persons of the same family or race.

NAME

NICKNAME

DATE

AGE

OCCASION

I WOULD DESCRIBE MYSELF AS . . .

MY FAMILY WOULD DESCRIBE ME AS . . .

WHAT I ATE FOR BREAKFAST THIS MORNING:

WHAT I'M WEARING TODAY:

WHAT I'M CURRENTLY WATCHING:

WHAT I'M CURRENTLY LISTENING TO:

WHAT I'M CURRENTLY READING:

THE LAST PERSON I TALKED TO:

_____

THE LAST PERSON I TEXTED:

_____

IF I COULD BE INTRODUCED TO ANYONE, I'D WANT TO MEET . . .

_____

IF I COULD GO ANYWHERE TOMORROW, I'D VISIT . . .

_____

SOMEDAY, I WANT TO . . .

_____

I'M MOST GRATEFUL FOR . . .

_____

MY FAVORITE FAMILY STORY:

_____

_____

_____

SOMETHING ABOUT THIS DAY I'LL ALWAYS REMEMBER:

_____

_____

_____

NAME

NICKNAME

DATE

AGE

OCCASION

I WOULD DESCRIBE MYSELF AS . . .

MY FAMILY WOULD DESCRIBE ME AS . . .

WHAT I ATE FOR BREAKFAST THIS MORNING:

WHAT I'M WEARING TODAY:

WHAT I'M CURRENTLY WATCHING:

WHAT I'M CURRENTLY LISTENING TO:

WHAT I'M CURRENTLY READING:

THE LAST PERSON I TALKED TO:

_____

THE LAST PERSON I TEXTED:

_____

IF I COULD BE INTRODUCED TO ANYONE, I'D WANT TO MEET . . .

_____

IF I COULD GO ANYWHERE TOMORROW, I'D VISIT . . .

_____

SOMEDAY, I WANT TO . . .

_____

I'M MOST GRATEFUL FOR . . .

_____

MY FAVORITE FAMILY STORY:

_____

_____

_____

SOMETHING ABOUT THIS DAY I'LL ALWAYS REMEMBER:

_____

_____

_____

NAME

NICKNAME

DATE

AGE

OCCASION

I WOULD DESCRIBE MYSELF AS . . .

_____

MY FAMILY WOULD DESCRIBE ME AS . . .

_____

WHAT I ATE FOR BREAKFAST THIS MORNING:

_____

WHAT I'M WEARING TODAY:

_____

WHAT I'M CURRENTLY WATCHING:

_____

WHAT I'M CURRENTLY LISTENING TO:

_____

WHAT I'M CURRENTLY READING:

_____

THE LAST PERSON I TALKED TO:

_____

THE LAST PERSON I TEXTED:

_____

IF I COULD BE INTRODUCED TO ANYONE, I'D WANT TO MEET . . .

_____

IF I COULD GO ANYWHERE TOMORROW, I'D VISIT . . .

_____

SOMEDAY, I WANT TO . . .

_____

I'M MOST GRATEFUL FOR . . .

_____

MY FAVORITE FAMILY STORY:

_____

_____

_____

SOMETHING ABOUT THIS DAY I'LL ALWAYS REMEMBER:

_____

_____

_____

NAME

NICKNAME

DATE

AGE

OCCASION

I WOULD DESCRIBE MYSELF AS . . .

MY FAMILY WOULD DESCRIBE ME AS . . .

WHAT I ATE FOR BREAKFAST THIS MORNING:

WHAT I'M WEARING TODAY:

WHAT I'M CURRENTLY WATCHING:

WHAT I'M CURRENTLY LISTENING TO:

WHAT I'M CURRENTLY READING:

THE LAST PERSON I TALKED TO:

_____

THE LAST PERSON I TEXTED:

_____

IF I COULD BE INTRODUCED TO ANYONE, I'D WANT TO MEET . . .

_____

IF I COULD GO ANYWHERE TOMORROW, I'D VISIT . . .

_____

SOMEDAY, I WANT TO . . .

_____

I'M MOST GRATEFUL FOR . . .

_____

MY FAVORITE FAMILY STORY:

_____

_____

_____

SOMETHING ABOUT THIS DAY I'LL ALWAYS REMEMBER:

_____

_____

_____

NAME

NICKNAME

DATE

AGE

OCCASION

I WOULD DESCRIBE MYSELF AS . . .

_____

MY FAMILY WOULD DESCRIBE ME AS . . .

_____

WHAT I ATE FOR BREAKFAST THIS MORNING:

_____

WHAT I'M WEARING TODAY:

_____

WHAT I'M CURRENTLY WATCHING:

_____

WHAT I'M CURRENTLY LISTENING TO:

_____

WHAT I'M CURRENTLY READING:

_____

THE LAST PERSON I TALKED TO:

_____

THE LAST PERSON I TEXTED:

_____

IF I COULD BE INTRODUCED TO ANYONE, I'D WANT TO MEET . . .

_____

IF I COULD GO ANYWHERE TOMORROW, I'D VISIT . . .

_____

SOMEDAY, I WANT TO . . .

_____

I'M MOST GRATEFUL FOR . . .

_____

MY FAVORITE FAMILY STORY:

_____

_____

_____

SOMETHING ABOUT THIS DAY I'LL ALWAYS REMEMBER:

_____

_____

_____

Día de los Muertos

On *Día de los Muertos*, or Day of the Dead,
in Mexico, families come together to joyfully
remember those ancestors who have gone
before them. They build altars decorated with
flowers and photos of their departed loved ones,
sometimes including favorite foods and personal
memorabilia to encourage spirits to visit.

NAME

NICKNAME

DATE

AGE

OCCASION

I WOULD DESCRIBE MYSELF AS . . .

_____

MY FAMILY WOULD DESCRIBE ME AS . . .

_____

WHAT I ATE FOR BREAKFAST THIS MORNING:

_____

WHAT I'M WEARING TODAY:

_____

WHAT I'M CURRENTLY WATCHING:

_____

WHAT I'M CURRENTLY LISTENING TO:

_____

WHAT I'M CURRENTLY READING:

_____

THE LAST PERSON I TALKED TO:

_____

THE LAST PERSON I TEXTED:

_____

IF I COULD BE INTRODUCED TO ANYONE, I'D WANT TO MEET . . .

_____

IF I COULD GO ANYWHERE TOMORROW, I'D VISIT . . .

_____

SOMEDAY, I WANT TO . . .

_____

I'M MOST GRATEFUL FOR . . .

_____

MY FAVORITE FAMILY STORY:

_____

_____

_____

SOMETHING ABOUT THIS DAY I'LL ALWAYS REMEMBER:

_____

_____

_____

NAME

NICKNAME

DATE

AGE

OCCASION

I WOULD DESCRIBE MYSELF AS . . .

MY FAMILY WOULD DESCRIBE ME AS . . .

WHAT I ATE FOR BREAKFAST THIS MORNING:

WHAT I'M WEARING TODAY:

WHAT I'M CURRENTLY WATCHING:

WHAT I'M CURRENTLY LISTENING TO:

WHAT I'M CURRENTLY READING:

THE LAST PERSON I TALKED TO:

_____

THE LAST PERSON I TEXTED:

_____

IF I COULD BE INTRODUCED TO ANYONE, I'D WANT TO MEET . . .

_____

IF I COULD GO ANYWHERE TOMORROW, I'D VISIT . . .

_____

SOMEDAY, I WANT TO . . .

_____

I'M MOST GRATEFUL FOR . . .

_____

MY FAVORITE FAMILY STORY:

_____

_____

_____

SOMETHING ABOUT THIS DAY I'LL ALWAYS REMEMBER:

_____

_____

_____

NAME

NICKNAME

DATE

AGE

OCCASION

I WOULD DESCRIBE MYSELF AS . . .

MY FAMILY WOULD DESCRIBE ME AS . . .

WHAT I ATE FOR BREAKFAST THIS MORNING:

WHAT I'M WEARING TODAY:

WHAT I'M CURRENTLY WATCHING:

WHAT I'M CURRENTLY LISTENING TO:

WHAT I'M CURRENTLY READING:

THE LAST PERSON I TALKED TO:

_____

THE LAST PERSON I TEXTED:

_____

IF I COULD BE INTRODUCED TO ANYONE, I'D WANT TO MEET . . .

_____

IF I COULD GO ANYWHERE TOMORROW, I'D VISIT . . .

_____

SOMEDAY, I WANT TO . . .

_____

I'M MOST GRATEFUL FOR . . .

_____

MY FAVORITE FAMILY STORY:

_____

_____

_____

SOMETHING ABOUT THIS DAY I'LL ALWAYS REMEMBER:

_____

_____

_____

NAME

NICKNAME

DATE

AGE

OCCASION

I WOULD DESCRIBE MYSELF AS . . .

_____

MY FAMILY WOULD DESCRIBE ME AS . . .

_____

WHAT I ATE FOR BREAKFAST THIS MORNING:

_____

WHAT I'M WEARING TODAY:

_____

WHAT I'M CURRENTLY WATCHING:

_____

WHAT I'M CURRENTLY LISTENING TO:

_____

WHAT I'M CURRENTLY READING:

_____

THE LAST PERSON I TALKED TO:

_____

THE LAST PERSON I TEXTED:

_____

IF I COULD BE INTRODUCED TO ANYONE, I'D WANT TO MEET . . .

_____

IF I COULD GO ANYWHERE TOMORROW, I'D VISIT . . .

_____

SOMEDAY, I WANT TO . . .

_____

I'M MOST GRATEFUL FOR . . .

_____

MY FAVORITE FAMILY STORY:

_____

_____

_____

SOMETHING ABOUT THIS DAY I'LL ALWAYS REMEMBER:

_____

_____

_____

NAME

NICKNAME

DATE

AGE

OCCASION

I WOULD DESCRIBE MYSELF AS . . .

_____

MY FAMILY WOULD DESCRIBE ME AS . . .

_____

WHAT I ATE FOR BREAKFAST THIS MORNING:

_____

WHAT I'M WEARING TODAY:

_____

WHAT I'M CURRENTLY WATCHING:

_____

WHAT I'M CURRENTLY LISTENING TO:

_____

WHAT I'M CURRENTLY READING:

_____

THE LAST PERSON I TALKED TO:

_____

THE LAST PERSON I TEXTED:

_____

IF I COULD BE INTRODUCED TO ANYONE, I'D WANT TO MEET . . .

_____

IF I COULD GO ANYWHERE TOMORROW, I'D VISIT . . .

_____

SOMEDAY, I WANT TO . . .

_____

I'M MOST GRATEFUL FOR . . .

_____

MY FAVORITE FAMILY STORY:

_____

_____

_____

SOMETHING ABOUT THIS DAY I'LL ALWAYS REMEMBER:

_____

_____

_____

outdooring

In Ghanaian culture, *outdooring* is a celebration that marks the first time an infant is taken out into the world. Typically taking place eight days after the birth, this is also the first time they are formally introduced to their extended family.

NAME

NICKNAME

DATE

AGE

OCCASION

I WOULD DESCRIBE MYSELF AS . . .

MY FAMILY WOULD DESCRIBE ME AS . . .

WHAT I ATE FOR BREAKFAST THIS MORNING:

WHAT I'M WEARING TODAY:

WHAT I'M CURRENTLY WATCHING:

WHAT I'M CURRENTLY LISTENING TO:

WHAT I'M CURRENTLY READING:

THE LAST PERSON I TALKED TO:

_____

THE LAST PERSON I TEXTED:

_____

IF I COULD BE INTRODUCED TO ANYONE, I'D WANT TO MEET . . .

_____

IF I COULD GO ANYWHERE TOMORROW, I'D VISIT . . .

_____

SOMEDAY, I WANT TO . . .

_____

I'M MOST GRATEFUL FOR . . .

_____

MY FAVORITE FAMILY STORY:

_____

_____

_____

SOMETHING ABOUT THIS DAY I'LL ALWAYS REMEMBER:

_____

_____

_____

NAME

NICKNAME

DATE

AGE

OCCASION

I WOULD DESCRIBE MYSELF AS . . .

MY FAMILY WOULD DESCRIBE ME AS . . .

WHAT I ATE FOR BREAKFAST THIS MORNING:

WHAT I'M WEARING TODAY:

WHAT I'M CURRENTLY WATCHING:

WHAT I'M CURRENTLY LISTENING TO:

WHAT I'M CURRENTLY READING:

THE LAST PERSON I TALKED TO:

_____

THE LAST PERSON I TEXTED:

_____

IF I COULD BE INTRODUCED TO ANYONE, I'D WANT TO MEET . . .

_____

IF I COULD GO ANYWHERE TOMORROW, I'D VISIT . . .

_____

SOMEDAY, I WANT TO . . .

_____

I'M MOST GRATEFUL FOR . . .

_____

MY FAVORITE FAMILY STORY:

_____

_____

_____

SOMETHING ABOUT THIS DAY I'LL ALWAYS REMEMBER:

_____

_____

_____

NAME

NICKNAME

DATE

AGE

OCCASION

I WOULD DESCRIBE MYSELF AS . . .

_____

MY FAMILY WOULD DESCRIBE ME AS . . .

_____

WHAT I ATE FOR BREAKFAST THIS MORNING:

_____

WHAT I'M WEARING TODAY:

_____

WHAT I'M CURRENTLY WATCHING:

_____

WHAT I'M CURRENTLY LISTENING TO:

_____

WHAT I'M CURRENTLY READING:

_____

THE LAST PERSON I TALKED TO:

_____

THE LAST PERSON I TEXTED:

_____

IF I COULD BE INTRODUCED TO ANYONE, I'D WANT TO MEET . . .

_____

IF I COULD GO ANYWHERE TOMORROW, I'D VISIT . . .

_____

SOMEDAY, I WANT TO . . .

_____

I'M MOST GRATEFUL FOR . . .

_____

MY FAVORITE FAMILY STORY:

_____

_____

_____

SOMETHING ABOUT THIS DAY I'LL ALWAYS REMEMBER:

_____

_____

_____

NAME

NICKNAME

DATE

AGE

OCCASION

I WOULD DESCRIBE MYSELF AS . . .

MY FAMILY WOULD DESCRIBE ME AS . . .

WHAT I ATE FOR BREAKFAST THIS MORNING:

WHAT I'M WEARING TODAY:

WHAT I'M CURRENTLY WATCHING:

WHAT I'M CURRENTLY LISTENING TO:

WHAT I'M CURRENTLY READING:

THE LAST PERSON I TALKED TO:

_____

THE LAST PERSON I TEXTED:

_____

IF I COULD BE INTRODUCED TO ANYONE, I'D WANT TO MEET . . .

_____

IF I COULD GO ANYWHERE TOMORROW, I'D VISIT . . .

_____

SOMEDAY, I WANT TO . . .

_____

I'M MOST GRATEFUL FOR . . .

_____

MY FAVORITE FAMILY STORY:

_____

_____

_____

SOMETHING ABOUT THIS DAY I'LL ALWAYS REMEMBER:

_____

_____

_____

NAME

NICKNAME

DATE

AGE

OCCASION

I WOULD DESCRIBE MYSELF AS . . .

MY FAMILY WOULD DESCRIBE ME AS . . .

WHAT I ATE FOR BREAKFAST THIS MORNING:

WHAT I'M WEARING TODAY:

WHAT I'M CURRENTLY WATCHING:

WHAT I'M CURRENTLY LISTENING TO:

WHAT I'M CURRENTLY READING:

THE LAST PERSON I TALKED TO:

_____

THE LAST PERSON I TEXTED:

_____

IF I COULD BE INTRODUCED TO ANYONE, I'D WANT TO MEET . . .

_____

IF I COULD GO ANYWHERE TOMORROW, I'D VISIT . . .

_____

SOMEDAY, I WANT TO . . .

_____

I'M MOST GRATEFUL FOR . . .

_____

MY FAVORITE FAMILY STORY:

_____

_____

_____

SOMETHING ABOUT THIS DAY I'LL ALWAYS REMEMBER:

_____

_____

_____

household ('haŭs-'hōld) *n.*

1.

Those who dwell under the same
roof and compose a family.

2.

A line of ancestry; a race or house.

NAME

NICKNAME

DATE

AGE

OCCASION

I WOULD DESCRIBE MYSELF AS . . .

MY FAMILY WOULD DESCRIBE ME AS . . .

WHAT I ATE FOR BREAKFAST THIS MORNING:

WHAT I'M WEARING TODAY:

WHAT I'M CURRENTLY WATCHING:

WHAT I'M CURRENTLY LISTENING TO:

WHAT I'M CURRENTLY READING:

THE LAST PERSON I TALKED TO:

_____

THE LAST PERSON I TEXTED:

_____

IF I COULD BE INTRODUCED TO ANYONE, I'D WANT TO MEET . . .

_____

IF I COULD GO ANYWHERE TOMORROW, I'D VISIT . . .

_____

SOMEDAY, I WANT TO . . .

_____

I'M MOST GRATEFUL FOR . . .

_____

MY FAVORITE FAMILY STORY:

_____

_____

_____

SOMETHING ABOUT THIS DAY I'LL ALWAYS REMEMBER:

_____

_____

_____

NAME

NICKNAME

DATE

AGE

OCCASION

I WOULD DESCRIBE MYSELF AS . . .

MY FAMILY WOULD DESCRIBE ME AS . . .

WHAT I ATE FOR BREAKFAST THIS MORNING:

WHAT I'M WEARING TODAY:

WHAT I'M CURRENTLY WATCHING:

WHAT I'M CURRENTLY LISTENING TO:

WHAT I'M CURRENTLY READING:

THE LAST PERSON I TALKED TO:

_____

THE LAST PERSON I TEXTED:

_____

IF I COULD BE INTRODUCED TO ANYONE, I'D WANT TO MEET . . .

_____

IF I COULD GO ANYWHERE TOMORROW, I'D VISIT . . .

_____

SOMEDAY, I WANT TO . . .

_____

I'M MOST GRATEFUL FOR . . .

_____

MY FAVORITE FAMILY STORY:

_____

_____

_____

SOMETHING ABOUT THIS DAY I'LL ALWAYS REMEMBER:

_____

_____

_____

NAME

NICKNAME

DATE

AGE

OCCASION

I WOULD DESCRIBE MYSELF AS . . .

MY FAMILY WOULD DESCRIBE ME AS . . .

WHAT I ATE FOR BREAKFAST THIS MORNING:

WHAT I'M WEARING TODAY:

WHAT I'M CURRENTLY WATCHING:

WHAT I'M CURRENTLY LISTENING TO:

WHAT I'M CURRENTLY READING:

THE LAST PERSON I TALKED TO:

_____

THE LAST PERSON I TEXTED:

_____

IF I COULD BE INTRODUCED TO ANYONE, I'D WANT TO MEET . . .

_____

IF I COULD GO ANYWHERE TOMORROW, I'D VISIT . . .

_____

SOMEDAY, I WANT TO . . .

_____

I'M MOST GRATEFUL FOR . . .

_____

MY FAVORITE FAMILY STORY:

_____

_____

_____

SOMETHING ABOUT THIS DAY I'LL ALWAYS REMEMBER:

_____

_____

_____

NAME

NICKNAME

DATE

AGE

OCCASION

I WOULD DESCRIBE MYSELF AS . . .

_____

MY FAMILY WOULD DESCRIBE ME AS . . .

_____

WHAT I ATE FOR BREAKFAST THIS MORNING:

_____

WHAT I'M WEARING TODAY:

_____

WHAT I'M CURRENTLY WATCHING:

_____

WHAT I'M CURRENTLY LISTENING TO:

_____

WHAT I'M CURRENTLY READING:

_____

THE LAST PERSON I TALKED TO:

_____

THE LAST PERSON I TEXTED:

_____

IF I COULD BE INTRODUCED TO ANYONE, I'D WANT TO MEET . . .

_____

IF I COULD GO ANYWHERE TOMORROW, I'D VISIT . . .

_____

SOMEDAY, I WANT TO . . .

_____

I'M MOST GRATEFUL FOR . . .

_____

MY FAVORITE FAMILY STORY:

_____

_____

_____

SOMETHING ABOUT THIS DAY I'LL ALWAYS REMEMBER:

_____

_____

_____

GROUP ACTIVITIES

· ◆ · ◆ ·

The following activities invite everyone to participate!
Complete them as a group with just your immediate family
or get your extended family to join in, too. The more, the
merrier! Find a moment when everyone is gathered together
to pull out the book, maybe after a big family dinner while
everyone is still at the table, or at a birthday or shower while
presents are being opened. Some activities work best if the
book is passed around, and others are meant to be read
aloud with the group shouting out answers for all to hear.

BIRTHDAY TIMELINE

◆ ◼ ◆

Keep track of everyone's special day!
Fill in this chart with every family member's birthday.

JANUARY	FEBRUARY

MARCH	APRIL

MAY	JUNE

JULY

AUGUST

SEPTEMBER

OCTOBER

NOVEMBER

DECEMBER

FAMILY SUPERLATIVES: ROUND 1

As a group, fill in which family member is . . .

. . . MOST LIKELY TO MAKE EVERYONE LAUGH OUT LOUD:

_____

. . . MOST LIKELY TO NOT GET THE JOKE BUT LAUGH ANYWAY:

_____

. . . MOST LIKELY TO WIN A BEST-DRESSED AWARD:

_____

. . . LEAST LIKELY TO BE WEARING MATCHING SOCKS:

_____

. . . MOST LIKELY TO NEED HELP FIXING THEIR COMPUTER:

_____

. . . MOST LIKELY TO HELP SOMEONE FIX THEIR COMPUTER:

_____

. . . MOST LIKELY TO KNOW WHAT SPORTS TEAMS ARE PLAYING ON TV:

_____

. . . LEAST LIKELY TO WANT TO COME BACK INSIDE:

_____

. . . MOST LIKELY TO HAVE THEIR NOSE IN A BOOK:

_____

. . . MOST LIKELY TO QUOTE POETRY AT THE DINNER TABLE:

_____

. . . MOST LIKELY TO MAKE THEIR OWN HALLOWEEN COSTUME:

_____

. . . LEAST LIKELY TO COLOR INSIDE THE LINES:

_____

OUR FAVORITE DISHES

◆

What foods appear on the table at every family gathering?
Are there any recipes that have been passed down for generations?
Have family members jot down their favorite foods in the plates
on these pages. Repeats are welcome! Tally them up and see what
dishes are the most popular.

ALL-TIME FAVORITES

_____

_____

_____

_____

_____

_____

_____

_____

_____

_____

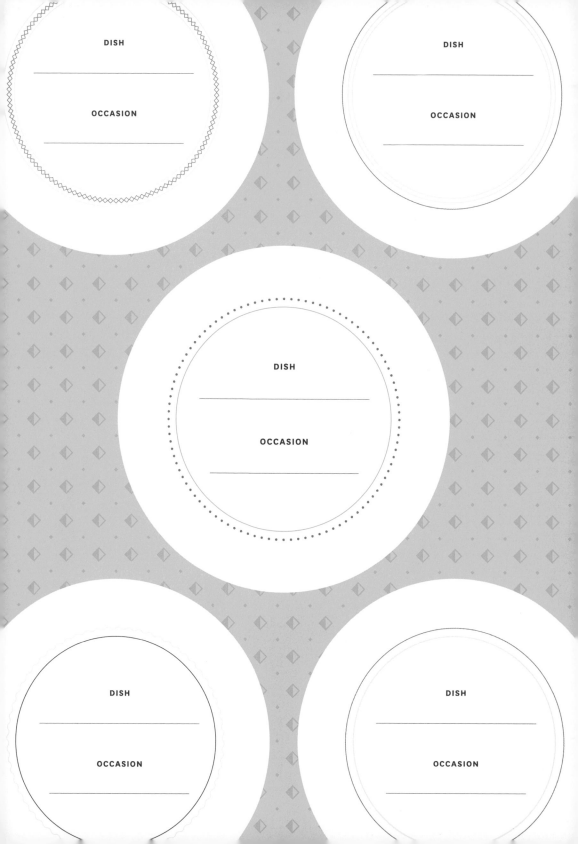

DISH
_____

OCCASION
_____

DISH
_____

OCCASION
_____

DISH
_____

OCCASION
_____

DISH
_____

OCCASION
_____

DISH
_____

OCCASION
_____

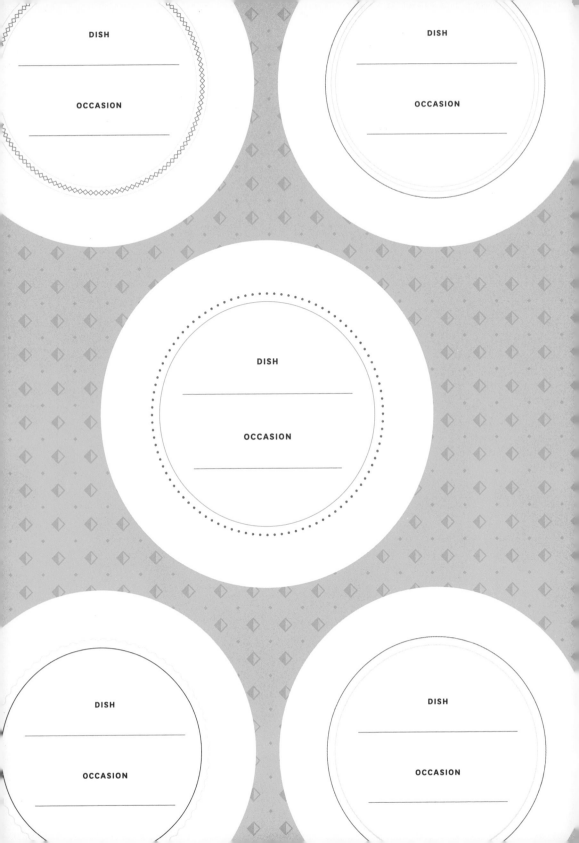

DISH

OCCASION

DISH

OCCASION

DISH

OCCASION

DISH

OCCASION

DISH

OCCASION

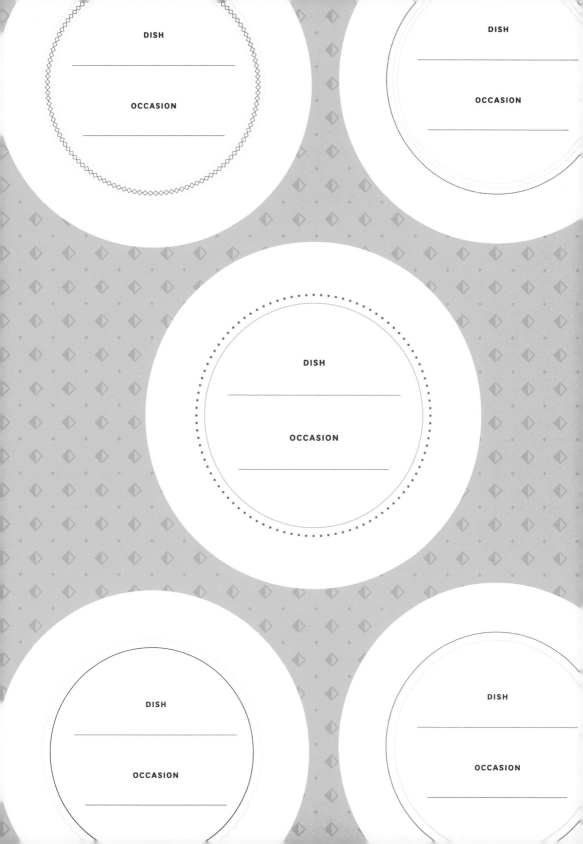

DISH

_____

OCCASION

_____

DISH

_____

OCCASION

_____

DISH

_____

OCCASION

_____

DISH

_____

OCCASION

_____

DISH

_____

OCCASION

_____

FUN FACTS: ROUND 1

As a group, write in which family member(s) . . .

. . . SPEAK(S) MORE THAN ONE LANGUAGE:

_____

. . . HAS/HAVE LIVED IN A FOREIGN COUNTRY:

_____

. . . KNOW(S) HOW TO DRIVE A MOTORCYCLE:

_____

. . . CAN HOTWIRE A CAR:

_____

. . . KNOW(S) HOW TO TAP DANCE:

_____

. . . CAN PLAY A MUSICAL INSTRUMENT:

_____

. . . PLAY(S) IN A BAND:

_____

. . . CAN DO A CARTWHEEL:

_____

. . . HAS/HAVE RUN A MARATHON:

_____

. . . PLAYED SPORTS IN COLLEGE:

_____

. . . HAS/HAVE SERVED IN THE MILITARY:

_____

. . . HAS/HAVE A GRADUATE DEGREE:

_____

. . . CAN ADD AND SUBTRACT IN THEIR HEAD:

_____

PARTY ANIMALS

◆

Reimagine your family as animals in a zoo. Who's the wise
elephant? The mischievous monkey? The fierce tiger?

HAVE EACH FAMILY MEMBER WRITE OR DRAW WHAT THEY WOULD BE IN THE SPACE BELOW.

FAMILY SUPERLATIVES: ROUND 2

As a group, fill in which family member is . . .

. . . MOST LIKELY TO BE IN CHARGE OF PLANNING A FAMILY GET-TOGETHER:

_____

. . . MOST LIKELY TO LOSE THEIR PHONE DURING A PARTY:

_____

. . . MOST LIKELY TO BE THE FIRST ONE ON THE DANCE FLOOR AT A FAMILY EVENT:

_____

. . . LEAST LIKELY TO FOLLOW THE RULES DURING A GAME NIGHT:

_____

. . . MOST LIKELY TO BRING SOMETHING HEALTHY TO A POTLUCK:

_____

. . . MOST LIKELY TO WANT TO EAT DESSERT FIRST:

_____

. . . MOST LIKELY TO FALL ASLEEP AFTER A BIG DINNER:

_____

. . . LEAST LIKELY TO BE ON TIME FOR A FAMILY GATHERING:

_____

. . . MOST LIKELY TO TELL AN EMBARRASSING STORY ABOUT THEIR KIDS:

_____

. . . MOST LIKELY TO START A STORY WITH "WHEN I WAS YOUR AGE":

_____

. . . MOST LIKELY TO KNOW WHAT THE LATEST FAMILY GOSSIP IS:

_____

. . . LEAST LIKELY TO FORGET SOMEONE'S BIRTHDAY:

_____

ONCE UPON A TIME . . .

Reimagine the family as cast of fairy-tale characters. Which one of
you is the brave knight? The clever sorceress? The fierce dragon?

HAVE EACH FAMILY MEMBER WRITE OR DRAW WHAT THEIR
FAIRY-TALE CHARACTER WOULD BE IN THE SPACE BELOW.

FUN FACTS: ROUND 2

As a group, write in which family member(s) . . .

. . . HAS/HAVE THE BEST TATTOOS:

_____

. . . LOVE(S) TO SING KARAOKE:

_____

. . . CAN WHISTLE LOUD ENOUGH TO GET EVERYONE'S ATTENTION:

_____

. . . KNOW(S) HOW TO DRAW AND/OR PAINT:

_____

. . . HAS/HAVE MET SOMEONE FAMOUS:

_____

. . . KNOW(S) THE MOST RANDOM TRIVIA:

_____

. . . HAS/HAVE BEEN SKYDIVING:

_____

. . . HAS/HAVE MARCHED IN A PROTEST:

_____

. . . CAN FIX ALMOST ANYTHING AROUND THE HOUSE:

_____

. . . KNOW(S) HOW TO MAKE EVERYONE SMILE:

_____

. . . HAS/HAVE THE MOST UNEXPECTED HIDDEN TALENT:

_____

Design by Melissa Faustine

ISBN: 978-1-4197-3389-5

Printed and bound in China
10 9 8 7 6 5 4 3 2 1

Abrams Noterie products are available at special discounts when purchased in
quantity for premiums and promotions as well as fundraising or educational
use. Special editions can also be created to specification. For details, contact
specialsales@abramsbooks.com or the address below.

ABRAMS The Art of Books
195 Broadway, New York, NY 10007
abramsbooks.com

MIX
Paper from
responsible sources
FSC
www.fsc.org   FSC™ C101537